This Is the Ark
That Noah Built

Shirley Neitzel / Illustrated by Benrei Huang

For Christine
—S. N.

For Jennifer and Bruce,
a special couple
and dear friends.
—B. H.

Large-quantity purchases or custom editions of this book are available at a discount from the publisher. For more information, contact the sales department at Augsburg Fortress, Publishers, 1-800-328-4648, or write to: Sales Director, Augsburg Fortress, Publishers, Box 1209, Minneapolis, MN 55440-1209.

ISBN 0-8066-4643-8

The paper used in this publication meets the minimum requirements of American National Standard for Information Sciences—Permanence of Paper for Printed Library Materials, ANSI Z329.48-1984. ♾ ™

Manufactured in China

08 07 06 05 04   1 2 3 4 5 6 7 8 9 10

God told Noah, kind and good,
to build an ark of gopher wood.

This is the ark that Noah built.

These are the donkeys, with hees and haws,
that went in the ark that Noah built.

These are the sheep, with frightened baas,
that followed the donkeys, with hees and haws,
that went in the ark that Noah built.

These are the lions, with deafening roars,
that lay by the sheep with frightened baas,
that followed the donkeys, with hees and haws,
that went in the ark that Noah built.

These are the mice with squeaks and snores,
that nuzzled the lions, with deafening roars,
that lay by the sheep, with frightened baas,
that followed the donkeys, with hees and haws,
that went in the ark that Noah built.

These are the silent and tall giraffes,
that straddled the mice with squeaks and snores,
that nuzzled the lions, with deafening roars,
that lay by the sheep, with frightened baas,
that followed the donkeys, with hees and haws,
that went in the ark that Noah built.

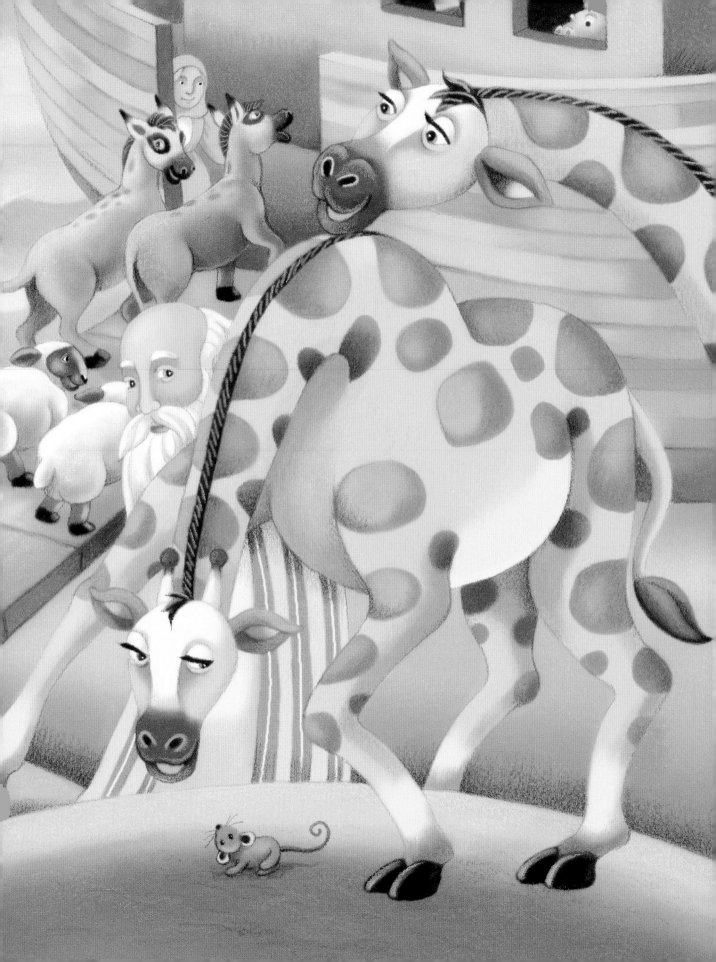

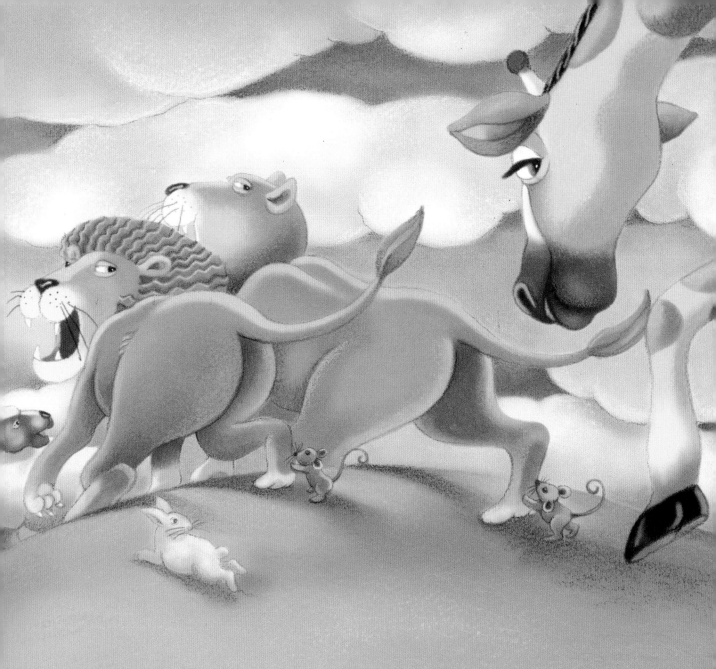

These are hyenas, with hearty laughs,
that crowded the silent and tall giraffes,
that straddled the mice, with squeaks and snores,
that nuzzled the lions, with deafening roars,
that lay by the sheep, with frightened baas,
that followed the donkeys, with hees and haws,
that went in the ark that Noah built.

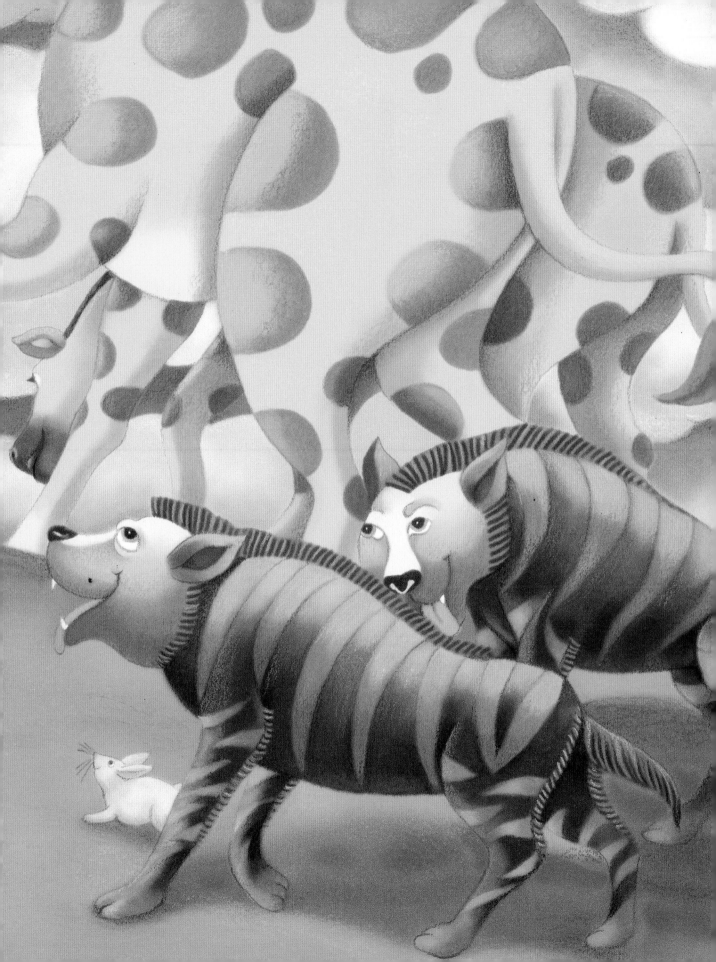

These are the monkeys, that chattered a lot,
that scolded hyenas, with hearty laughs,
that crowded the silent and tall giraffes,

that straddled the mice, with squeaks and snores,
that nuzzled the lions, with deafening roars,
that lay by the sheep, with frightened baas,
that followed the donkeys, with hees and haws,
that went in the ark that Noah built.

These are the elephants, that never forgot,
that nudged the monkeys, that chattered a lot,
that scolded hyenas, with hearty laughs,
that crowded the silent and tall giraffes,

that straddled the mice, with squeaks and snores,
that nuzzled the lions, with deafening roars,
that lay by the sheep, with frightened baas,
that followed the donkeys, with hees and haws,
that went in the ark that Noah built.

These are tortoises, quiet and slow.
When they were in, Noah said, "Let's go!
The ark is full from rafters to floor."
Then his wife and sons helped shut the door
as they went in the ark that Noah built.

It rained forty days, and poured every night,
until all the land disappeared from sight.

Then Noah sent doves to fly over the sea.
One brought back a branch from a green olive tree.
Noah cried, "Hallelujah!" and brushed off a gnat,
as the ark came to rest on Mount Ararat.

"Noah," God said, "you've obeyed my command.
Never again will I flood all the land.
That is my promise. Remember it by
the rainbow I've placed high in the sky."

Then with squeaks, and bleats, and happy laughs,
mice, sheep, hyenas, and silent giraffes,
elephants, monkeys, and donkeys came trooping,
down the gangplank, shrieking and whooping.
Lions pranced and practiced their roars,
and slow-footed tortoises crept out the doors,
and off of the ark that Noah built.

Family Activities for the Ark That Noah Built

Prayer

Dear God,
Thank you for animals and plants
*   that live in our world of wonders.*
Thank you for sunshine,
*   and rain, and rainbows.*
And thank you for giving your promise.
Amen.

Things to Do

We see rainbows when light shines through water in the air.

- Look for a rainbow when the sun shines after the rain.
- Make a rainbow by standing with your back to the sun and spraying water from a garden hose.
- Blow bubbles. Dip a drinking straw in water mixed with dishwashing soap. Look for the rainbow in the bubbles before they burst.
- Draw a picture of a rainbow with all seven colors in this order: red, orange, yellow, green, blue, indigo, and violet. The red should be on the outside of the arc and the violet inside.
- Remember the order of the colors of the rainbow by reciting this silly sentence:
  Real old yaks gallop best in vests.

Things to Make

Lion and Lamb Mobile

You will need:
2 paper plates
markers or crayons
glue, pencil, and scissor
cotton balls stretched and flattened
yarn cut into pieces about 2 ½ inches long

Directions:
Draw a lion's face on the back of one paper plate.
Draw a lamb's face on the back of the other paper plate.
Color the faces.
Glue yarn around the lion's face covering the edge of the plate.
Glue cotton around the lamb's face.
Punch a hole in the top of each plate and hang them,
    back to back, by a string.

Paper Bag Donkey Puppet

You will need:
lunch-size paper bag
construction paper
pencil, glue, and scissors
yarn

Directions:
Draw and cut a donkey face on construction paper.
Cut eyes, nostrils, and ears. Glue them in place. Add yarn for a mane.
Put glue on the bottom of the bag.
Place the face on the glue so the muzzle hangs over the edge.
Trace the muzzle to make a bottom jaw.
Glue the bottom jaw along the inside fold of the bag.
Glue or color a red mouth on the jaw.
Put your hand in the bag to make your donkey "talk."

Did you know . . . ?

No one is really sure what **gopher wood** is. It might be cypress or wood sealed with pitch to make it waterproof.

Most **donkeys** are slow, but some wild ones run 40 miles per hour—as fast as racehorses.

When a **sheep** eats grass, it stores it in one part of its stomach. Then later it brings the food back to its mouth where it is chewed again! The sheep is chewing its cud.

An adult female **lion** walks through tall grass carrying its tail high in the air. A black tuft on the end of its tail makes it easy for the cubs to follow.

Mice have sharp front teeth that grow all their lives. They can even gnaw wood without ruining their teeth.

Giraffes have seven bones in their necks—the same as people do.

A **hyena's** laugh doesn't mean it's happy. That's the way it howls.

Many **monkeys** can pick up things with their feet as easily as with their hands, because their big toes work like thumbs.

Elephants don't get stuck in mud. Spongy pads on their feet spread out when they step down and get smaller when they lift them.

Tortoises don't have teeth. They bite with strong, horny jaws.

Doves feed their young "pigeon milk," food they have swallowed, partially digested, and regurgitated or coughed up!